AMERICAN DIPLOMACY IN THE EUROPEAN WAR

BY

MUNROE SMITH

PROFESSOR OF JURISPRUDENCE, COLUMBIA UNIVERSITY

REPRINTED FROM POLITICAL SCIENCE QUARTERLY
Vol. XXXI, No. 4, December, 1916

NEW YORK
PUBLISHED BY GINN & COMPANY
1916

In the interest of creating a more extensive selection of rare historical book reprints, we have chosen to reproduce this title even though it may possibly have occasional imperfections such as missing and blurred pages, missing text, poor pictures, markings, dark backgrounds and other reproduction issues beyond our control. Because this work is culturally important, we have made it available as a part of our commitment to protecting, preserving and promoting the world's literature. Thank you for your understanding.

CONTENTS

		PAGE
I.	Neutrality or discrimination	481
II.	Preparations for defense	484
III.	Restraints of trade	488
IV.	Submarine warfare	494
	"Cruiser" warfare	495
	Armed merchantmen	498
	Unrestricted warfare	500
	Interception of contraband	503
V.	Right of retaliation	505
VI.	Mistakes and omissions	509
VII.	The munitions trade	513
	Conclusions	518

AMERICAN DIPLOMACY IN THE EUROPEAN WAR

THERE has been no little dissatisfaction in the United States with the conduct of our diplomacy in the present world war. There are those who maintain that we should have espoused the cause of one or of the other group of belligerents. Both among these citizens and in the far larger body supporting the policy of neutrality, there are many who maintain that our government has failed to protect, as effectively as it could and should have protected, the rights of American citizens as neutrals and as non-combatants.

I. *Neutrality or discrimination*

Those opposing the policy of neutrality, or advocating a more or less unequal or discriminating neutrality, are divided by their sympathies, or by their views of national duty in international relations, into two groups. On the one side it is asserted that we should have protested against the invasion of Belgium, and that we should not have embarrassed the conduct of the war, on the part of Great Britain and its allies, by insisting upon the rights of neutral trade. A smaller number claim that the Entente Allies so clearly represent the cause of liberty and of civilization that we should from the outset have joined our armed forces to theirs. Of those who sympathize with the Central Empires or feel antipathy to British imperialism, none, so far as I know, has claimed that we should have taken up arms on the Teutonic side; but many assert that we should have met British restraint of neutral commerce, not with protests only, but with retaliatory action, by placing an embargo upon all trade with Great Britain and its allies, or at least upon the export of munitions of war. By many of those demanding that the export of military supplies be prohibited, it is indeed denied that such action would be unneutral; it is asserted, on the contrary, that under existing circumstances this export is unneutral. This last contention will be examined later.[1]

In so far as these divergent demands represent racial sympathies, they are, from the American point of view, deplorable and dangerous. In a country like ours, inhabited by people of many diverse origins, it would be fatal to internal peace and progress to permit our foreign policy to be controlled by any such influences. In so far, however, as these demands embody a sense of the solidarity of world interests and a feeling that a wrong committed against one nation is an injury to all nations; in so far as they are based upon a belief that international morals will never become international law in any proper sense of the word until the sanction of force—force of arms or force of economic discrimination—is employed by nations not directly and selfishly concerned to uphold the international order by punishing its assailants—in so far these demands deserve respectful consideration. They represent the lines of progress on which at some future period a durable world-order may be attained. Under present conditions, however, the maintenance of the peace and order of the world will hardly be secured by accepting the principle that it is the right and duty of every nation to support international right and to penalize international wrongs. So long as it is left to each nation to determine where the right lies in any controversy, divergent sympathies and interests will tend to produce opposing decisions; and anything approaching general action under the proposed principle might widen any war into a world war.

A special reason why the United States should have protested against the violation of Belgian neutrality is found by some of our citizens in the fact that the invasion of Belgium was not only a violation of international law but also a breach of treaties, and that, among the treaties by which the integrity of Belgium was safeguarded, there was one, a Hague convention concerning

[1] *Cf. infra*, pp. 513-518.

the rights of neutral states, to which the United States was a party. Assuming what many international lawyers deny, that this convention was in force at the moment when Germany demanded for its armies a right of way through Belgium,[1] it may be pointed out that in such conventions or resolutions of international congresses it is not generally assumed that the signatory powers bind themselves to act, either singly or collectively, against any one of their number that may violate the convention. It should further be remembered that, in the Hague conferences and in other international congresses in which our government has participated, it has repeatedly stated that it is contrary to our traditional policy to intervene in any European political question.

In view of these facts it can hardly be maintained that our government was bound to protest against the invasion of Belgium. It of course had the right to protest, independently of its adhesion to the Hague convention, against a clear and admitted violation of international law. The objections to sending such a protest to the German government were, first, that under existing diplomatic practice it is so unusual for a state to protest against any action which does not affect its own rights and interests or those of its citizens, that our protest might reasonably have been viewed as an unfriendly act; and second, and this is perhaps the more important consideration, that it was and is difficult to see what practical object could have been attained by a formal protest. On the very day on which the German troops entered Belgium, the German Chancellor publicly admitted that Germany's action was illegal, that it was a wrong for which Germany hoped later to afford full compensation. An American protest would either have been met by a repetition of this confession and by the Chancellor's original plea of national necessity, or it would have elicited those accusations against the Entente Allies and the Belgian government which the German authorities advanced at a later period and which

---

[1] The dispute turns mainly upon the very debatable question whether Great Britain, which had not ratified this particular convention, was or was not virtually a belligerent on August 2, 1914.

were intended to show that Belgium was not in fact a neutral state. Either answer would have terminated the incident; the latter answer by raising questions of fact which could not have been profitably discussed in diplomatic correspondence.

Personally, I feel that the view of Germany's conduct toward Belgium that was taken by the great majority of the American people should have been expressed by our administration, not indeed by a direct protest to the German government, but in another way, presently to be indicated.

In considering the general attitude that our government should have taken towards the belligerent powers, it must not be forgotten that, in a democratic country, any important action on the part of the government must be supported by public opinion; and that, if it is a question of taking sides in a war at the risk of being drawn into the war, any policy that deviates from strict neutrality must be approved by a very large majority of the people. To have taken the side of the Central Empires would assuredly not have commanded such support; and it seems highly improbable that our government would have received anything like general support in espousing or clearly favoring the cause of the Entente Allies.

II. *Preparations for defense*

Assuming that our government, under all the circumstances, was bound to remain neutral, and that its neutrality was not to be discriminatory, it is still open to question whether it acted with the degree of foresight, of energy and of consistency which was requisite for the effectual protection of its citizens as neutrals and as non-combatants. Any such inquiry may of course be discredited by insisting on the proverbial superiority of hindsight. Such an objection, however, taken without limitation, would effectually bar all criticism of political conduct. It is of course unfair to demand that our government should have foreseen the incalculable or even the improbable. It is quite fair, however, to maintain that it should have foreseen the probable, to say nothing of the inevitable.

It is a matter of common knowledge that in every great war the interests of the belligerents come into conflict with the interests and traditional rights of neutrals. It is also a matter of common knowledge that in international relations national rights are maintained in last instance by force, and that any state that hopes to secure recognition of its rights must be prepared to enforce them to the utmost of its ability. At the outbreak of the present war, the neutral states of continental Europe promptly mobilized their armies. Had Belgium possessed a militia comparable in efficiency to that of Switzerland, it is at least doubtful whether the Germans would have found that the quickest and easiest road into France led through that neutral country.

The geographical position of the United States protects it from the immediate perils against which Holland and Switzerland found it advisable to take arms; but with the outbreak of the war between Germany, France and England, it was obvious that conditions would recur similar to those that prevailed a century ago in the great naval struggles of the Revolutionary and Napoleonic period. It was obvious, after the British ultimatum of August 4, 1914, that the war would be waged in part at least on the high seas, and that the interests and rights of neutral commerce would be jeoparded. Under these circumstances, is it not clear that our government should have taken measures for the defence of our rights at sea analogous to those that Holland and Switzerland took for the defense of their territorial integrity?

It seems obvious that the President should have called Congress together, at the earliest possible date after the outbreak of the war, and should have asked for an appropriation to mobilize our navy—to put our war ships, as regarded personnel and equipment, into a state of complete efficiency. Such a proposal could have raised no partisan question. The necessity of such a step is shown by the fact that, in the last session of Congress, we were told by our naval experts that our fleet was still short of men, to say nothing of battle cruisers and scout ships.

During the last two years the connection between diplomacy and preparation for eventual war has been drastically illustrated in our own experience. When, in the second year of the war, the President began to urge adequate preparation for national defense, he asked his fellow citizens, in a public address delivered in a western city, whether they wished him to go on writing notes because there was nothing else he could do. When, after this agitation, he sent to the German government, last April, what really proved to be, this time, an ultimatum, the American note elicited from the German press, among other comments, the statement that the extent and vehemence of our demands was ludicrously disproportionate to our effective military and naval strength. Another German paper put it more succinctly: it said that the United States was brandishing a wooden sword. The really pathetic appeal of the President and the not unmerited sneers of the German journalists might have been forestalled by prompter action.

It seems obvious, again, that at such a special session of Congress the President might well have asked for power to meet invasions of our rights as neutrals and as non-combatants by placing an embargo upon exports to any offending country.

Had our government, at the beginning of the war, obtained the means necessary to make our naval force effective and, at the same time, authority to put economic pressure upon any state that might violate or impair the rights of our citizens, it is highly probable that some at least of the complications in which we were subsequently involved might have been avoided.

If, at the outbreak of the war, the President had felt moved to express the sentiment of a large part of our people regarding the violation of Belgian neutrality, such a special session would have afforded a fit opportunity, and the presidential message to Congress would have been the proper vehicle. An expression of the President's view of foreign affairs, in a message to Congress, is a matter primarily if not solely of American concern, with which no foreign state has any reason to occupy itself. A precedent could have been found in the fact that President Monroe employed this method of expressing American feeling, not only regarding the struggle between Spain and its American colonies, but also regarding the struggle between Turkey and its Hellenic subjects. If a president of the United States may express officially his sympathy with a European people striving to obtain independence by insurrection, surely he may express sympathy with a European people whose independence is illegally assailed. If President Wilson had based a request for the mobilization of the navy and for power to lay an embargo upon exports, not only upon general considerations—on the menace to neutral commerce necessarily resulting from a great naval war—but also and particularly upon the flagrant disregard of neutral rights and of treaty obligations with which the war had opened, and upon the probability that the wrong already committed would draw in its train, by way of retaliation, further and perhaps equally serious illegalities, he would have freed his own and the nation's conscience in a manner wholly unexceptionable, even from the point of view of existing international practice.

Simultaneously with the calling of a special session of Congress for the purposes above indicated, it would have been proper and wise to open negotiations with other neutral maritime states for joint deliberation and possible joint action in the assertion and maintenance of neutral rights at sea. It is said that such a step was considered by our State Department, but that it was deemed inadvisable to take it, for fear that we might be led by other states into action not in our interest. If this be really the ground on which our inaction was based, our State Department displayed a singular misconception of the nature of international coöperation. Any association of states is governed, like the old Polish Diet, by the rule of unanimity. At the same time, in spite of the theoretic equality of all participants, the influence of the several states in any international association is largely proportionate to their power, as was also the case in the Polish Diet, where the few magnates usually had their way. By our failure to initiate any such coöperation of neutrals, we lost an opportunity to render an important service to the world and also to increase the moral influence of our own country.

It may be objected that such a program as has been outlined, however desirable, could hardly have been carried through early in the war without serious discord in the ranks of the party in power, perhaps not without disruption of the cabinet.

The well-known view of the then Secretary of State, that preparation for war rather promotes than averts conflict, would certainly have led him to oppose the plan of mobilizing our navy, and he might possibly have found support from one or more of his colleagues. It seems probable, however, that if the Secretary had resigned upon this issue, his action would have commanded little more popular support than it received in the following summer, when he resigned because our case against unrestricted submarine warfare was to be seriously pressed. Had the Secretary resigned in the autumn of 1914, when his unfitness for his post had already been demonstrated by eighteen months' trial, the peril to party cohesion would hardly have been more serious than it proved in the following summer, and the advantage to the administration would have been even greater.

III. *Restraints of trade*

It is not the purpose of this paper to consider all the questions with which our diplomacy had to deal during the first two years of the war—a task which would demand a volume—nor is it necessary, in touching upon the chief questions, to go fully into their more technical aspects. On some questions final judgment can hardly be rendered until the diplomatic correspondence is published in full, and until more exact knowledge is obtainable regarding disputed matters of fact. In its main lines, however, the policy followed by our government is well known. The task imposed upon it was to defend, so far as was practicable, the interests of our citizens; to find tenable grounds on which its remonstrances and demands could be based; and to use the means best adapted to secure the ends at which it aimed. How satisfactorily it has performed this task during the past two years seems neither an illegitimate nor a premature inquiry.

The first serious attack upon neutral shipping interests was the planting of submarine mines beyond the limits of territorial waters. According to the British contention, Germany initiated this proceeding early in the war, by planting mines in the English Channel. In retaliation, on November 3, 1914, Great

Britain declared the North Sea "a military area" and announced that it had planted mines in that sea. It is alleged, however, that British mines were placed in that sea, outside of the limit of territorial waters, long before the "military area" proclamation. Against these proceedings our government entered no protest. We should, I think, have addressed protests to both powers. Our failure to make any such protest has proved the more unfortunate, because mines imperil not only the property of neutrals but also the lives of non-combatants. This is the case at least with the German mines. British control of the sea enables that power to offer to neutral vessels, if they are permitted to cross the North Sea at all, safe conduct by expert pilots to neutral ports. Germany can offer no such security. Our tacit admission that the planting of mines in the open sea is permissible has proved an embarrassment to us in our controversy with Germany regarding the employment of submarines against merchant vessels. Whenever it is uncertain whether a merchant vessel, even a vessel under the American flag, has been sunk by a submarine or by a mine, we are estopped from protest.

Our controversies with Great Britain have resulted from its attempt to suppress the entire import and export trade of its enemies—an attempt which necessarily involves the checking of all neutral trade with the Central Powers. It is not maintained, except by the Germans, that the object pursued by Great Britain is illegal. It is a legitimate measure of war to attempt to reduce an enemy country to submission by cutting off its supplies, including food supplies. We ourselves followed this course in our struggle against the Southern Confederacy. Prince Bismarck, after his retirement from office, inspired in the Hamburg newspaper that he used as his organ of publicity an article in which he pointed out that, if Germany should be involved in war with enemies of superior naval strength, they would assuredly attempt to cut off all importation of foodstuffs. He did not indicate that such an attempt would be illegal or even inhumane. His object was to urge the German government to give greater encouragement to German agriculture, and particularly to grain-growing.

It is, however, maintained that the methods adopted by the Entente Allies to cut off all trade with the Central Empires are illegal. At the outset, the British government sought to realize its purpose by so expanding its contraband lists as to include nearly everything that Germany needed. It declared foodstuffs contraband, justifying this action on the ground that in Germany all foodstuffs had been brought under governmental control. By the Order in Council of March 11, 1915, it developed a new type of blockade. This order forbids voyages to or from German ports. It also authorizes the detention of vessels sailing to neutral ports and carrying goods with an enemy destination or which are enemy property; also the detention of vessels sailing from neutral ports and carrying goods which are of enemy origin or are enemy property. In the order itself these measures are stated to be retaliatory; but in the official correspondence and in unofficial British pamphlets it is maintained that they are a legitimate extension of blockade, adapted to modern and special conditions. They constitute an attempt to blockade the entire German Empire, partly by blockading Germany's ports in the North Sea, and partly by stopping all neutral trade with Germany that passes through the North Sea and the neutral countries of Holland, Denmark, Norway and Sweden. In so far as goods consigned to these countries are concerned, Great Britain invokes the "ultimate destination" rule, which was set up by our courts in our similar attempt to stop all trade with the Southern Confederacy; but it goes much further than we did in shifting the burden of proof, in assuming that goods consigned to Germany's neighbors are intended to be forwarded to Germany. In more than one respect the British blockade lacks the characteristics of a legitimate blockade as heretofore recognized. As far as the Baltic ports of Germany are concerned there is no blockade. Hence the blockade does not operate uniformly against all neutral countries. It is effective against all countries whose trade with Germany passes through the North Sea, against Spain, the United States and the Latin-American states, but it is not effective as regards the exportation of Dutch, Danish, Norwegian or Swedish products to Germany, by land or across the Baltic. It is similarly ineffective as regards the exportation of Swiss products to Austria and to Germany. To a certain extent the Entente Allies are able to check trade between the Central Empires and their neutral neighbors by limiting imports to these neighbors, by permitting them to import only such goods and such quantities of goods as are apparently necessary for their own consumption. They are "rationed"; and they are not permitted to replace by importation goods of their own production which they export to Germany or to Austria. This, however, involves an unprecedented interference not only with the trade but with the domestic economy of these neutral states—an interference which is practicable only because of their comparative weakness.

What directly concerns us is that our trade with the Central Empires is cut off, and our trade with the neutral neighbors of these empires limited, by measures of at least doubtful legality. If they constitute an extension of the law of blockade, they seem to us to stretch this law to the breaking-point.

On the other hand, it should be noted that, in all cases where neutral commerce is subjected to restraint not clearly authorized by international law, the British government does not impose the penalties which attach to an attempted breach of blockade or to the carrying of contraband. Unless goods destined for Germany are absolute contraband, neither the vessel nor the cargo is forfeited. The vessel is regularly released after unloading in a British port. The goods are requisitioned by the government or sold in open market or ultimately released. In case of requisition or sale, the owners are either compensated or are promised compensation at the close of the war.

This whole system is obviously illogical. If the British measures in restraint of neutral trade are legitimate, action contrary to these measures should entail the customary penalties. If, on the other hand, these measures are illegitimate, they should not be enforced. It is, however, one of the strong points of the English that, in matters of conduct, they have the courage to disregard logic. They consider interests, general and individual, and they take general sentiment into account. So far as is consistent with the attainment of their purposes, they avoid injury to interests and offense to sentiment. The course which the British government has pursued has undoubtedly minimized the injury that its sweeping restraints inflict upon neutral trade and the resentment which these restraints necessarily excite.

It should be noted, further, that the British prize courts have apparently reverted to Lord Stowell's theory, that they are not bound to apply Orders in Council if these are clearly inconsistent with the recognized rules of international law. And back of these courts lies, as is recognized by the British government, ultimate recourse to international arbitration.

It is to be noted, finally, that the British Order in Council of March 11 and the identical French Decree of March 12, 1915 are, by their express terms, acts of retaliation against the German "war zone" proclamation of February 4, 1915. The effect of reprisals upon neutral rights is, however, a matter demanding special and separate consideration.[1]

Against Great Britain's action our government has repeatedly protested. In our protest against the Order in Council of March 11, our State Department said, March 30, 1915:

> The Order in Council of the 15th[2] of March would constitute, were its provisions carried into effect as they stand, a practical assertion of unlimited belligerent rights over neutral commerce within the whole European area and an almost unqualified denial of sovereign rights of the nations now at peace.

Other and more recent controversies between our government and the British government turn on the detention and examination of postal matter carried on neutral ships, and on the "blacklisting" of neutral traders. As regards the first of these matters, our government insists that the action of Great Britain is unwarranted by previous international practice and constitutes a distinct breach of the Hague Convention of 1907. As regards the second issue—raised by the action of the British government in forbidding its subjects to trade with designated neutral persons and firms, because the trade of these persons

[1] *Cf. infra*, pp. 505-509.

[2] The date given by our State Department is that of the British note enclosing and explaining the order.

and firms with Great Britain's enemies is asserted to be a channel through which an indirect trade between Great Britain's subjects and its enemies may be conducted—our government insists that these British measures operate within our territory and in the territory of other neutrals as an unfair and illegal restraint of trade. In neither of these matters has our government failed to formulate its protests, and all the questions involved have been kept open for final adjustment.

It has been persistently maintained by the Central Empires, and it is asserted by many of our own writers and speakers, that our government should have gone further—that it should have asked Congress for authority to impose a retaliatory embargo upon exports, or at least upon exports of military supplies, to the offending countries.

Here, again, we are confronted with the practical question whether such a policy would have received general support among the American people. In the early part of the war it would have been welcomed by our cotton growers and by other producers who had previously enjoyed an important trade with the Central Empires. Before long, however, many of these producers found that the increased demands of other European countries more than made up for the loss of the Teutonic markets. The steel industry and all industries that were or could be engaged in the production of military supplies found, almost from the beginning of the war, that the unprepared Entente Allies were anxious to purchase their products at almost any price. The profits derived from increasing sales at rising prices of those agricultural and industrial products that were needed in Europe stimulated the domestic demand for other products. For the most part, accordingly, American producers were directly or indirectly benefited. Had our government undertaken to close to American exports, or to a very large portion of these exports, the markets of Great Britain, France and Russia, when these powers had already closed the Central European markets, it would have inflicted upon the country a degree of economic injury for which no administration could have assumed the responsibility.

Against an embargo upon the export of military supplies

there were other objections, based not on American economic interests but on the equitable claims of belligerent states and the vital interests of peaceful peoples. These objections will be considered later, in examining the charge that, in the matter of the munitions trade, America's attitude has been unneutral.[1]

The conduct of our diplomacy as regards Great Britain and its allies is, I think, fairly defensible. It has not seemed to our government either necessary or expedient to meet the restrictions placed by these states on our trade with retaliatory restrictions which, in harming them, would also harm ourselves. It has seemed sufficient to file our protests as a basis for subsequent claims. After the war the British government may concede that its measures were irregular; and the rules of international law will then be vindicated. Great Britain may be the readier to do this, because in future it may need these rules for the protection of its own trade. It may the more easily do this, because its action is claimed to be retaliatory.

IV. *Submarine warfare*

Between the United States and Germany there were, and are, far more serious controversies. In dealing with our protracted dispute with Germany regarding submarine warfare, it is necessary to make a sharp distinction between questions which arose and were discussed simultaneously and which at times appeared to be confused. We must distinguish between the so-called "cruiser warfare" and warfare conducted by sinking belligerent merchant vessels without warning.

The use of submarines in war is a novelty. As late as 1899 it was proposed, at a Hague conference, that their use be forbidden in war. This proposal failed; it was maintained that for the weaker states the submarine might prove a necessary weapon of defense. At that time, however, no employment of submarines was advocated or anticipated except against enemy war vessels. In a memorandum submitted to our government March 8, 1916, the German Ambassador stated, and quite correctly, that the submarine was "a new weapon, the use of which

[1] *Cf. infra*, pp. 513 518.

had not yet been regulated by international law." From this premise he drew the amazing conclusion that, in using this new weapon, Germany " could not and did not violate any existing rule." This latter statement is of course untrue. In the use of a new weapon a belligerent nation may unquestionably violate well-recognized rules of international law. The armored tractor cars recently introduced by the British, for example, are new weapons, the use of which has not been regulated by international law; but it does not follow that Great Britain could lawfully use these new weapons to destroy enemy field hospitals. In the use of its submarines Germany has violated rules quite as well established as those which protect military hospitals.

In using its submarines against merchant ships, Germany in fact invokes established rules of international law. It claims for submarines the rights accorded to cruisers. Cruisers have the right to capture enemy vessels and neutral vessels carrying contraband. Whenever it is impossible or even inexpedient to take a captured vessel into any of the captor's home ports for condemnation, it is permissible to sink it. Due provision, however, must always be made for the safety of the non-combatants, the crew and any passengers.

Inasmuch as the employment of submarines against merchant vessels was without precedent, it was open to the United States government to question the legitimacy of so using them. I think that we should have contested this point, because the submarine is not fitted to do cruiser work. In using the cruiser against merchant vessels, a captured vessel may exceptionally be sunk; in using the submarine the captured vessel must always be sunk. The exception ceases to prove the rule; it supplants the rule. Even if the captor's home ports be not blockaded, as are Germany's, the submarine is not able to put prize crews on captured vessels, nor is it able, without serious risk to itself, to convoy such vessels to a home port. What is of much more consequence, in sinking a captured merchant vessel the submarine is unable, in the vast majority of cases, to make proper provision for the safety of the non-combatants. At the best, it can only permit them to embark in open boats, without regard to weather or distance from land.

In the President's address to Congress, April 19, 1916, and in the note, commonly known as the "Sussex" note, which was simultaneously delivered by our Ambassador in Berlin to the German Foreign Office, it is asserted that our government took this position from the outset. The following passage is to be found in both documents:

It has therefore become painfully evident that the position which this government took at the very outset is inevitable, namely, that the use of submarines for the destruction of an enemy's commerce is of necessity, because of the very character of the vessels employed and the very methods of attack which their employment of course involves, incompatible with the principles of humanity, the long-established and incontrovertible rights of neutrals and the sacred immunities of non-combatants.

As a matter of fact this position was first taken in the first "Lusitania" note, May 13, 1915. Before this we had practically acquiesced in the use of submarines for the visitation, search and capture of merchant ships. Not only had we made no protest against such use, but in the note of February 20, 1915, which was addressed to both groups of belligerents, and in which we endeavored to induce them to make mutual concessions, one of our proposals was "that neither will use submarines to attack merchant vessels except to enforce the right of visit and search." In the first "Lusitania" note, our demand was that the submarine should visit, like a cruiser, and should not sink without warning; and all that was said about the impropriety of such visitation was *obiter dictum*. In the second American note on submarine warfare, June 9, 1915, there was no allusion to the illegality or inhumanity of the use of submarines to visit and search merchant vessels. Our demand was still that the submarine should visit, not sink without warning. And in the third American note on the subject, July 21, 1915 —a note written after the German government had so far yielded to our remonstrances as to direct the commanders of its submarines to observe the rules of cruiser warfare—our State Department said:

The events of the past two months have clearly indicated that it is possible and practicable to conduct such submarine operations as have characterized the activity of the Imperial German Navy within the so-called war zone in substantial accord with the accepted principles of regulated warfare.

In the note sent by our State Department to Great Britain and its allies in January 18, 1916, in which it was suggested that the practice of arming merchant vessels be discontinued, the use of submarines against an enemy's commerce was defended, " since those instruments of war have proved their effectiveness in this practical branch of warfare."

Even in the " Sussex " note of last April, in which our government reverted to its earlier position regarding the use of submarines for visit and search, all that is said on this point is again *obiter;* for the demand is that submarine warfare shall be conducted, so far as possible, according to the rules of cruiser warfare. And in the German note of May 5, which our government found satisfactory, the German government undertakes only " that merchant vessels . . . shall not be sunk without warning and without saving human lives, unless the ship attempts to escape or offers resistance." Our government has accordingly accepted, as satisfying the demands of legality and of humanity, the giving to the non-combatants of " that poor measure of safety," as our State Department has described it, which is to be found in small open boats on the high seas.

In conceding the legitimacy of the employment of submarines against merchant vessels, so long as the rules of cruiser warfare are observed, our government has virtually recognized the right of Germany to capture by its submarines and to sink, not only belligerent vessels, but also neutral vessels, if after visit and search these are found to contain contraband, even conditional contraband. Of this alleged right, which other and weaker neutrals contest, Germany has made extensive use. Up to the end of October, 1916, it had destroyed, according to Norwegian statements, one-seventh of the Norwegian merchant marine. The reason it is not exercising this alleged right against us is that the relations between Germany and the United States are governed in this matter by the Prussian-American treaties of July 11, 1799 and May 1, 1828. Under these treaties, as interpreted by our State Department, Germany is not entitled to destroy our vessels carrying contraband; as interpreted by the German Foreign Office, however, these treaties do not impair Germany's right to destroy such vessels, but impose upon the Imperial government the duty of paying in each case for vessel and cargo. This difference of opinion is to be submitted to arbitration. Meanwhile, " in order to furnish to the American government evidence of its conciliatory attitude," the German government has promised not to destroy American vessels carrying conditional contraband, but reserves the right to destroy such vessels if they carry absolute contraband.[1]

The activities of one or more German submarines off our coast in the autumn of the present year indicate the possibility that something like a blockade of our ports might conceivably be maintained by this class of war vessels; and so long as the Germans conform to the rules of cruiser warfare as interpreted by our State Department, our government seems estopped from raising any objections. The only question open is whether Germany is or is not free to sink American ships carrying absolute contraband, subject to liability for the value of the vessels and their cargoes.

The admission on the part of our government that submarines may be employed to visit, search and capture merchant ships, belligerent or neutral, has proved extremely embarrassing in the discussion of the status of armed merchantmen. According to existing international law, a merchantman has the right to carry mounted guns and to use them to resist capture. If it makes use of its armament, it becomes a combatant and may lawfully be sunk in the combat; but the fact that it carries guns for defense does not convert it into a warship.

These rules, as Germany contends, grew up under conditions

[1] See the correspondence regarding the sinking of the "William P. Frye," March 31, 1915 to Sept. 15, 1915. The fact that the Prussian-American treaties covered the case does not seem to have been appreciated by our State Department until the German Foreign Office pointed it out. German diplomacy doubtless welcomed the opportunity to show Germany's scrupulous adherence to treaty obligations.

that no longer prevail. They were established when piracy was rife; they were perpetuated during the period when privateering was admissible. In recent times, when merchantmen have been threatened with capture only by regular warships, their right to resist capture has not been invoked or used. Accordingly, the German authorities argue, this right, which has long ceased to be reasonable, has been lost by disuse. Armed merchantmen should therefore be treated as warships. The German government claims that British merchantmen in particular should be so treated, because, as they allege, Great Britain has armed some at least of its merchant vessels not for defense but for aggression. Proof of this purpose is found in instructions alleged to have been issued to British merchant captains, directing them to fire upon any German submarine that approaches them.

The Entente Allies maintain, on the other hand, that the only reason why the right of merchantmen to resist capture has not been employed in recent times is that resistance to regular warships had become hopeless. The fragility of the submarine, the fact that it may be sunk by a single shot, has again changed the situation, and the ancient right of defense may legitimately be exercised against this new type of warship. Denying, as they do, that submarines may lawfully be used to visit, search or capture merchantmen, the Entente Allies assert that the attempt so to use a submarine, its mere approach, is an act of unlawful aggression; that the merchantman thus approached may at once use against the submarine any weapon it possesses; and that such action is defensive.

So long as Germany claimed and exercised the right to sink enemy merchantmen at sight and without warning, whether these were armed or unarmed, the status of the armed merchantman was a matter of little immediate importance. When Germany and Austria announced that the commanders of their submarines had been instructed to observe the rules of cruiser warfare against enemy merchantmen, provided these were not armed for offensive purposes against German or Austrian submarines, the status of the armed merchantman became a burning question.

In the note of January 18, 1916, sent to Great Britain and its allies, our State Department endeavored to bring about an agreement between the belligerent powers, by which the Central Empires should definitively abandon the practice of sinking unarmed merchantmen without warning, and Great Britain and its allies should waive their right to arm their merchant vessels. In this note our government stated that it was

> impressed with the reasonableness of the argument that a merchant vessel carrying armament of any sort, in view of the character of submarine warfare and the defensive weakness of undersea craft, should be held to be an auxiliary cruiser. . . .

Such an agreement as our State Department was endeavoring to negotiate would have involved the recognition by Great Britain and its allies that submarines could legitimately be employed to visit, search and capture merchant vessels. Failing to obtain the suggested agreement, our State Department reverted to the position that the existing rules of international law regarding armed merchantmen must be observed. Such a position is defensible, but it can hardly be expected that Germany should regard it as reasonable. In his note of January 18, Secretary Lansing himself said that

> if a submarine is required to stop and search a merchant vessel on the high seas . . . it would not seem just nor reasonable that the submarine should be compelled, while complying with these requirements, to expose itself to almost certain destruction by the guns on board the merchant vessel.[1]

Had our government consistently maintained the position it occasionally took, that submarines should not undertake cruiser warfare against merchantmen because they can not observe cruiser rules, the risk they run in trying to observe these rules could have been cited in support of its argument.

The most acute controversy between our government and

[1] The risk that submarines run in attempting to stop and search merchantmen is appreciably diminished when the submarines hunt in couples. Even if a merchantman succeeds in destroying one of its assailants, it is almost certain to be sunk by the other.

that of Germany began with the German Admiralty proclamation of February 4, 1915, in which notice was given that the waters surrounding Great Britain and Ireland were to be treated as a "war zone"; that after February 18 enemy merchant ships might be destroyed without making provision for the safety of their crews and passengers; and that neutral ships might be exposed to the same peril. The German government disclaimed any intent to attack neutral vessels, but indicated that such attacks might be made by mistake, particularly in view of the fact that British vessels were making use of neutral flags.

The protest raised by our government, in its note of February 10, dealt primarily with the menace to neutral shipping. Our warning that the German government would be held to "a strict accountability" for the destruction of American vessels or the lives of American citizens did not clearly indicate that we should insist upon that accountability if American lives were lost in the sinking of belligerent merchant ships. The note could be so interpreted; but it was equally capable of being interpreted in the opposite sense. That the prime solicitude of our government at that time was to avert the possible destruction of American ships and their crews is indicated by the fact that, on the same day, February 10, it asked the government of Great Britain to forbid the use by British vessels of the American flag. To this request the British government declined to accede.

In one instance, an American vessel, the "Gulflight," was sunk, May 1, by a German submarine, and several American lives were lost. In other instances American vessels were attacked: the "Cushing," April 28, by an aeroplane; the "Nebraska," May 25, by a submarine. In its note of February 16, replying to the American note of February 10, the German Foreign Office defended the "war zone" proclamation as a legitimate reprisal against various illegal acts and practices of the British government; explained that it had given neutral shipping due warning; and stated that neutral vessels disregarding this warning "bear their own responsibility for any unfortunate accidents." This position it abandoned May 11, promising that if a neutral ship, even a ship carrying contraband, should be sunk without warning, "the German government will unreservedly recognize its responsibility therefor." This change of attitude was perhaps occasioned by the energetic reaction of American public sentiment against the sinking of the "Lusitania," May 7. It may well have seemed wise to sacrifice a weak if not indefensible position in order not to complicate the defense of a position which seemed stronger.

The promise of the German government to make compensation for the sinking of neutral ships without warning was not accepted by our government as a satisfactory adjustment of the controversy raised by the "war zone" proclamation. In the first "Lusitania" note, May 13, our State Department said:

Expressions of regret and offers of reparation in case of the destruction of neutral ships sunk by mistake, while they may satisfy international obligations, if no loss of life result, cannot justify or excuse a practice, the natural and necessary effect of which is to subject neutral nations and neutral persons to new and immeasurable risks.

The controversy raised by the sinking of the British steamer "Falaba," March 28, in which one American citizen lost his life, and by the sinking of the "Lusitania," in which more than one hundred Americans perished, continued until May 5, 1916. At some time in the summer of 1915, the German government issued to its submarine commanders an order not to sink "liners" without warning. The sinking, without warning, of the liner "Arabic," July 9, by which more American lives were sacrificed, was regretted and disavowed October 5, and the German Ambassador informed our State Department that the orders issued by the Emperor to the commanders of German submarines "have been made so stringent that the recurrence of incidents similar to the 'Arabic' case is considered out of the question." Subsequent to the sinking of the "Arabic," however, similar incidents occurred, in which the submarines attacking passenger steamers without warning were acknowledged either by the Austro-Hungarian or by the Turkish government to be sailing under their respective flags; and on March 24, 1916, the British channel steamer "Sussex" was sunk by a German submarine without warning and with further sacrifice of American lives. The American note of April 18, which the President read to Congress and which ended with a definite threat of the severance of diplomatic relations, elicited the German note of May 5, in which the controversy was shelved rather than settled by the pledge that the orders given to German submarine commanders, "not to sink merchant vessels without warning and without saving human lives, unless the ship attempt to escape or offer resistance," should be maintained and enforced until further notice. There is, in this note, no reservation of the right to sink armed enemy vessels, nor is there any waiver of such a right; this phase of the question is simply ignored. The diplomatic victory of the United States, if victory it be, is limited to the securing of a sort of armistice as regards unarmed merchantmen.

In the controversy between the two governments on this matter—eliminating the question of the status of armed merchantmen—the right to sink enemy merchantmen without warning was based by the German government on two grounds: the right of retaliation, and the right of a belligerent to intercept its enemy's military supplies.

As regards the latter point, the German case may fairly be stated as follows. It is not disputed by the German government that the usual and recognized method by which a belligerent intercepts contraband destined for its enemies is by visit, search and capture. Even when the merchantman carrying contraband is an enemy vessel, it is the usual practice to visit the vessel in order to determine its nationality. Because of the fragility of the submarine, however, it is unsafe for it to attempt to observe this practice where an enemy merchant vessel is concerned, and especially dangerous when such a vessel carries munitions of war, which it is naturally expected to defend, if defense be possible. When the vessel attacked is known to be an enemy vessel—and there was no doubt of the identity of the "Lusitania"—and when the fact that it is carrying ammunition is known—and in the German note of May 28, 1915, it is asserted that the "Lusitania" had on board no less than 5400 cases of ammunition—there is really no need of visit or search. Not having cruisers on the high seas, and being forced to rely on its submarines, Germany, as Count Bernstorff put it, adapted its method of warfare to the "peculiarity" of its new weapon. This entire line of argument is summed up in the German note of May 28, 1915, in one sentence:

The German government feels that it acts in just self-defense when it seeks to protect the lives of its soldiers by destroying munitions destined for the enemy *with the means of war at its command*.[1]

The position taken by our government on this question was, from the outset, substantially the same that it finally took upon the question of the right of a submarine to sink an armed merchantman without warning.[2] Our State Department has consistently refused to admit that the introduction of a new weapon automatically changes the rules of international law. Until the law is changed by general acquiescence or by express convention, the new weapon must be used in compliance with existing rules. If it is unable to do any particular kind of military work without overriding these rules, it should not attempt such work. On the question of the use of the submarine against an unarmed enemy vessel, this position is not only legally tenable, but highly reasonable. The results which the German submarines have obtained under the system of cruiser warfare indicate that the "Lusitania," which was not armed, could have been arrested by warning shots; that its captain could have been forced, under threat of immediate destruction of his vessel, to put its crew and passengers into boats; and that the liner could then have been sunk without any such sacrifice of life as resulted from its destruction without warning. Had the "Lusitania" summoned assistance by wireless, this would have been an act of resistance, and its immediate destruction would have been legitimate—in so far, at least, as submarine warfare against merchantmen can be regarded as legitimate.

In the later German notes this justification of unrestricted submarine warfare—the necessity of intercepting military supplies destined for Germany's enemies—is not emphasized. In

---

[1] Italics are the writer's.
[2] *Cf. supra*, p. 500.

the note of May 5, 1916, it is not mentioned. The German government concentrates its defense upon the right of reprisal.

V. *Right of retaliation*

The justification of the "war zone" proclamation as an act of retaliation or reprisal has not, in my judgment, been satisfactorily traversed by our State Department. Its failure to find the proper answer to this plea is the more regrettable, because in this war nearly every breach of law by either group of belligerents has been based, in whole or in part, on the right of reprisal. In so far as the reasoning contained in its notes can be disengaged from their somewhat rhetorical form, the position of our government seems to be that reprisal may be legitimate as against an enemy that is violating the rules of international law, but that the reprisal must not injure neutrals. In its note of March 30, 1915, to the British government, protesting against the Order in Council of March 11, our State Department says that the British plea of retaliation is doubtless to be interpreted as

> merely a reason for certain extraordinary activities on the part of His Majesty's naval forces and not as an excuse [for] or prelude to any unlawful action. If the course pursued by the present enemies of Great Britain should prove to be in fact tainted by illegality and disregard of the principles of war sanctioned by enlightened nations, it cannot be believed, and this Government does not for a moment believe, that His Majesty's Government now wish the same taint to attach to their own action or would cite such illegal acts as in any sense or degree a justification for similar practices on their part in so far as they affect neutral rights.

In its note of July 21, 1915, to the German government, our State Department asserts that "a belligerent act of retaliation is *per se* an act beyond the law, and the defense of an act as retaliatory is an admission that it is illegal." So sweeping an assertion is quite indefensible. Reprisal is a right sanctioned by international law, and an act of retaliation so sanctioned is not *per se* beyond the law. The grain of truth in this utterance is that, when a belligerent invokes the right of reprisal, he admits that *except for the right of reprisal* his action would be illegitimate. Here again, what our government really asserts is that the right of reprisal cannot be invoked in support of any act that injures neutrals. In the first "Lusitania" note, our State Department refuses to admit that measures of retaliation "operate in any degree as an abbreviation of the rights of American shipmasters, or of American citizens bound on lawful errands as passengers on merchant ships of belligerent nationality." Again, in the note of July 21, 1915, it is said that acts of reprisal "are manifestly indefensible when they deprive neutrals of their acknowledged rights."

If these statements assume, as they seem to assume, that the rights of neutrals are determinable without taking any account of the belligerent right of reprisal, they simply beg the question. Neutral rights are in some degree abridged when they come into collision with belligerent rights. How far they are abridged in any particular case is a question of international law. In international law it is well settled that if a legitimate act of war on the part of a belligerent state, directed primarily against its enemies, inflicts incidental injury upon the persons or property of neutrals, neither those neutrals nor the states to which they owe allegiance have a right to raise protest or demand satisfaction. And since international law authorizes reprisals, a legitimate reprisal is *per se* a legitimate act of war. In order to find any ground for protest, the protesting state must show that the particular reprisal of which it complains is illegitimate. To do this involves a much more careful examination of the law of reprisal, and of the limits within which the right of reprisal may be exercised, than our State Department has attempted to make.

It is clear that reprisal must be based on a prior violation of international law by the adversary. The assertion on the part of a belligerent that his adversary has been guilty of illegal conduct does not bar neutrals incidentally injured from inquiring into the truth of such an assertion. In our controversy with Germany regarding the "war zone" proclamation, however, we could not question the truth of the German assertion that Great Britain had violated international law, since we had repeatedly made the same assertion.

It is clear that any act of reprisal must be directed primarily against the enemy, not against a neutral. The German invasion of Belgium would not have justified a British invasion of Holland by way of retaliation; nor did it justify the Entente Allies in invading Greek territory. Whatever justification may be plead for this latter act, it is not to be found in the right of reprisal. Similarly, Germany's breaches of international law gave Great Britain no right that it did not previously possess to place restrictions on neutral trade with Germany; nor did the British restraint of such trade, however illegal, give Germany any right that it did not previously possess to interfere with neutral vessels trading with Great Britain. Here again, whatever justification may be found for the action of either belligerent, none can be found in the right of reprisal. The sinking of the "Lusitania" and of the "Sussex," on the other hand, were acts primarily directed against an enemy of Germany; and unless these acts were illegitimate as against that enemy, they did not become illegitimate simply because citizens of a neutral country were passengers on those enemy vessels.

It is claimed, indeed, that there is a difference, as regards the exercise of the right of reprisal, between land warfare and sea warfare. If in the present war an American were killed by a bomb dropped by a French aeroplane upon Karlsruhe, in reprisal against German action in dropping bombs on an undefended French city, our government would assuredly have no ground of complaint against the French government. When, however, an attack is made upon a belligerent steamer on the high seas, and this attack is of such a character that except for the right of reprisal it would be illegal, the situation is alleged to be different; and the fact that there are neutral passengers on the steamer is asserted to make the attack illegitimate so far as they are concerned. This distinction is based primarily upon the assertion that any German city belongs to Germany, while the seas belong to all men. The "Lusitania," however, was legally British territory. A second ground for the distinction is found by our State Department in the fact that the American passengers on the "Lusitania" were exercising their right to travel on their lawful errands. Waiving possible questions as to the nature and content of a "right to travel," it is clear that in embarking on the "Lusitania" they placed themselves under British jurisdiction and became "temporary subjects" of Great Britain. It is hard to see how their position and rights can be differentiated from those of an American citizen traveling on his lawful errands within Germany's territorial jurisdiction. The legal position of the American passengers on the "Lusitania" seems indistinguishable from that of the British passengers, and their rights, as against Germany, were not American rights, nor even neutral rights, but non-combatants' rights.

It is clear, however, that there must be some limits to the exercise of the right of reprisal. I venture to suggest that such limits are to be found in a comparison between the alleged offense and the attempted reprisal as regards their respective degrees of illegality and of inhumanity. In the interest of the world, it must be recognized that belligerents are not permitted to overbid each other in illegality and in inhumanity. This should not be permitted even as between belligerents; for otherwise, through reprisal and counter-reprisal, each exceeding the other in barbarity, war would inevitably revert to its most primitive form, and there would be nothing to prevent a final burning of prisoners at the stake. Nor should overbidding be permitted in reprisals which tend to injure neutrals. An act of reprisal must not involve a more serious impairment of neutral rights than the alleged offense for which the reprisal is taken. For otherwise, through reprisal and counter-reprisal, all neutral rights might eventually disappear in such a world war as is now raging.

If our government had taken this position, it would, I think, have enlisted the support of all neutrals, and its suggestions would probably have been accepted, at least after the establishment of peace, by all the countries now at war. And it would have found a clear and tenable ground on which to protest against the German "war zone" proclamation. Applying the principle suggested, it could have said to Germany: Your proposal to sacrifice non-combatant lives and to endanger the lives of neutrals is not a legitimate retaliation for any measure, however illegal, which Great Britain has adopted; for the taking of life is no proper retaliation for the taking of goods.

There is some evidence that the principle which I am endeavoring to formulate was, at least subconsciously, in the minds of Americans and Germans alike. In seeking to justify its "war zone" proclamation, Germany has tried to show that its retaliation was not disproportionate to its enemy's offense. It has tried to place British restraints upon neutral commerce on the same plane with its own destruction of non-combatant lives at sea, by alleging that the purpose of the British measures is to inflict upon millions of non-combatants death by starvation. It is, however, highly improbable that the British government now expects or ever expected to accomplish any such result, any more than the North, in the War of the Rebellion, expected to destroy the population of the Southern States by starvation. In such cases, the real expectation is that, by cutting off imports of food, the blockading power may inflict upon the people of the blockaded country such privations as may weaken their fighting spirit. The Germans themselves tell us, and with apparent truth, that such a result as the starvation of the German people cannot be attained by the most effective blockade of their Empire. Under these circumstances, their retaliation is disproportionate. It inflicts immediate death upon non-combatants by drowning, because of a purpose attributed to the enemy, which Germany itself says cannot be realized, to destroy German non-combatants by starvation.

The principle here suggested, the application of the proportional test to the offense and the reprisal, seems also to be recognized in many of the utterances of our State Department. In the first "Lusitania" note, our government asserts that the natural and necessary effect of the German measures of retaliation is " to subject neutral nations to new and immeasurable risks." Our government has further insisted, throughout its controversy with Germany, on the impossibility of placing on the same plane economic injury and the sacrifice of life.

VI. *Mistakes and omissions*

The conduct by our government of its controversy with the German government is open to serious criticism. Its protests and demands have been substantially justifiable, but the grounds on which they have been based have not always been wisely chosen. This is notably the case as regards its position in the matter of reprisals. In other matters our government seems to have taken its initial attitude without full consideration of all the aspects of the problems presented, and without prevision of the logical and necessary consequences of its first decision. In some of these matters it was forced later to shift its ground, which gave to its conduct an appearance of vacillation. In some instances, as a result of unnecessary and inadvisable concessions, as in the matter of submarine warfare against merchant vessels, it has been obliged to make its final stand, as in the matter of armed merchantmen, on grounds that are far from satisfactory.

Our government has been criticised, and with reason, for its failure promptly to support its protests against German action either with action or with the threat of definite action. Between the German "war zone" proclamation and the note in which the German Foreign Office promised that its submarines should observe the rules of cruiser warfare until further notice, there was a stretch of fifteen months, filled with repeated losses of American lives and repeated notes of protest. Whether it be true or untrue that in the spring of 1915 the then Secretary of State gave the Austro-Hungarian Ambassador to understand that the language of our first notes was intended chiefly for home consumption; whether the belief of the Teutonic diplomatists that our government was not likely to take any decisive action was or was not based on any official assurances or intimations; it is clear that until the spring of 1916 the notes of our State Department were not taken very seriously. In order to account for this result, or lack of result, it is not necessary to assume that either of the current allegations just noticed is true. The fact that our government went on sending notes, without action or threat of definite action, sufficiently accounts for such a belief.

It is not disputed that there is, as the President and the Secretary of State have repeatedly pointed out, not only in notes to the German Foreign Office but also in open letters and in speeches to the American public, a very great difference between our controversies with Great Britain and those with Germany. It is the difference between illegal restraint of neutral trade and illegal destruction of neutral lives. Economic losses can to some extent be made good; human life is inestimable. A government can not discuss indefinitely what it regards as the illegal killing of its citizens. It cannot submit controversies of this character to arbitration unless, pending arbitration, it can obtain a stay of killing. The situation is precisely the same that arises in controversies between individuals when irremediable damage is being inflicted. In such cases municipal law authorizes the complainant, pending the judicial determination of all questions in dispute, to demand an injunction.

At the time when the controversy aroused by the German "war zone" proclamation was becoming acute, the administration would probably have received very general support in taking any action that seemed necessary to protect American lives. Germany's conduct of the war in general; its treatment of the Belgian people, and in particular (because in this instance there was no dispute regarding the facts) the exaction of heavy contributions from Belgian cities whose trade had been destroyed; an inept and irritating propaganda, conducted by semi-official German agents; conspiracies, suspected although not yet proven, to prevent, by criminal methods, the manufacture and export of American munitions of war—these and other circumstances were arousing, even before the German naval administration opened an unrestricted warfare against belligerent merchant vessels, a stronger and more general anti-German feeling than had existed at the outbreak of the war. During the spring and summer of 1915 anti-German feeling in the United States apparently reached its highest point. It was diminished later by growing resentment at British invasions of neutral and in particular of American rights, notably by British interference with postal correspondence and by the British blacklist. In May, 1915, our government had indisputable ground for action in the sinking, without warning, of American vessels; and the anger aroused by the sacrifice of American lives in the sinking of the "Lusitania" would have insured general support of any action short of a declaration of war—possibly even of such action.

What effective action, however, could our government have

taken? The rupture of diplomatic relations, which it first definitely threatened a year later, seemed to many Americans undesirable. Its effects, so far as Germany was concerned, would have been purely moral; and it would have had the practical result of terminating the activities of American agents in relieving the necessities of the Belgian people as well as the good offices of our embassies in the Central Empires in their surveillance of detention camps and military prisons. A declaration of war, even had it been supported by American public opinion, would have been inadvisable in our state of military and naval unpreparedness. If, as was said, Germany could not have waged effective war against us, neither could we have waged war effectively against Germany. Moreover, conditions in Mexico seemed not unlikely to call for the full exercise of such effective military strength as we possessed. During the past summer and autumn, although we were nominally not at war with Mexico, nearly all our available military forces were sent into that country or were stationed on its northern frontier.

An embargo upon a non-existent trade may, on its face, seem absurd; but if the President had obtained from Congress, early in the war, the power to prohibit exports to any country that should disregard our rights as neutrals, it seems probable that an intimation that this power might be used against the Central Empires would have produced no slight effect. An embargo upon American exports to the Central Empires would at once relieve the British and French governments of a very considerable portion of the work that they are now doing in cutting off supplies from those empires; and if such an embargo were imposed upon our exports to their enemies, our government could very properly coöperate with them in making our embargo effective. We could utilize all the machinery which they have devised for preventing American goods from entering Germany through the neighboring neutral states. What would perhaps seem even more important to the German government, such coöperation between the United States and the Entente Allies would remove, for the time, the chief occasions of friction between them—friction which the Central Empires probably still regard, and certainly regarded in the spring of 1915, as a valuable asset of their diplomacy. If at the moment when the German embassy at Washington was warning the American people by newspaper advertisements that the "Lusitania" might be sunk, that embassy had been notified that the President would retaliate for the sacrifice of any American lives by prohibiting all trade with the Central Empires, it is probable that the "Lusitania" would have reached its port unmolested. It is even more probable, it is almost certain, that the threat of an embargo, then or later, would have secured at a much earlier date all that was obtained by the ensuing year's diplomatic correspondence.

VII. *The munitions trade*

Although the unrestricted submarine warfare on commerce conducted by Germany and its allies seemed to our government more obviously illegitimate than the restrictions imposed on neutral trade by Great Britain and its allies, and although the injuries inflicted upon American citizens by the Central Empires seemed far graver than any for which Great Britain and France were responsible, the attitude of our government was substantially the same towards both belligerent groups. It omitted no word to Germany or to Great Britain that seemed adapted to secure the recognition of the rights of American citizens, and it took no action against either power for the enforcement of those rights. Under these circumstances it is somewhat surprising that our government should be charged, as it has been and is charged by the governments of the Central Empires and by their adherents in the United States, with unneutral conduct, because it did not take action to compel Great Britain to abandon its illegal measures. Those who make this charge do not hesitate to explain what action our government should have taken: it should have prohibited the export of munitions of war.

Before this action was demanded for the purpose just indicated, it was demanded on the ground that, under existing circumstances, the American manufacture and export of military supplies was unneutral. It was not asserted that international law imposes upon a neutral state any duty to prevent or restrict such exports. It was claimed, however, that international equity required such action on the part of the United States. It was claimed that we should have taken cognizance of the fact that the Central Empires were unable to import military supplies from over sea, and that our export of such supplies was solely to their enemies. It is fair to sell to all belligerents, but unfair to sell to one side exclusively. It was also pointed out that in most wars there are numerous neutral states from which belligerents may draw military supplies; it is ordinarily not a question whether a belligerent shall buy such supplies, but where he shall buy them; whereas in this world war the United States is the only important industrial country at peace, and consequently its citizens enjoy a practical monopoly of the business in question. This fact, it was urged, made it especially unfair that they should be permitted to sell to one group of belligerents exclusively. It was asserted, finally, that the scale upon which the manufacture of military supplies was organized in this country, after the outbreak of the war, was in conflict with the spirit of neutrality. It was not a question of continuing trade previously established, but of developing what practically amounted to a new industry. When this new industry was organized for the service of one group of belligerents exclusively, the country in which it was organized became practically a base of military operations against the other group.

If, however, the spirit of neutrality required that we should consider the situation of the different belligerents and discriminate in the interest of fair play, is it not obvious that we were bound to consider the whole situation? In addition to the fact that the Central Empires could not draw military supplies from us, were we not entitled and bound to consider the fact that they stood in no such need of arms and munitions as did the Entente Allies? When an armed man attacks an unarmed adversary, the fight, to ordinary human sentiment, is not a fair fight. A similar feeling is aroused when a nation, prepared for war to an extraordinary and unprecedented degree, attacks an ill-prepared neighbor. This, it will be said, is sheer sentimentality; but is the opposite position wholly rational? Is it reason, or is it sentiment, that asserts that Germany and Austria were entitled to take every advantage of their superior preparation for warfare on land, but that we should not have permitted Great Britain and France to draw any advantage, of which we could deprive them, from their superior naval preparation and their resultant control of the sea?

Again, were the Entente Allies not justified in anticipating that any temporary shortage of military supplies could be made good in part by imports; and if our government had made it impossible for them to buy such supplies in the only neutral market which the war had left open to them, would not its action have been justly regarded by them as unfair? And if it be admitted that an unprepared nation is entitled to draw military supplies from neutral countries, does it not follow that it is entitled to draw all it needs?

In the Austrian note of June 29, 1915, in which the argument against the American export of military supplies is elaborated, it is assumed that the established rule, according to which a neutral power is not bound to prevent the export of military supplies to a belligerent, is based entirely on the equities of the neutral manufacturers, who are not to be deprived of "the export trade that was theirs in time of peace." The equities of ill-prepared belligerents are entirely ignored.

Considering the entire situation, we may well assert that our government, in following the letter of the law, observed its spirit also. If this conclusion be not accepted, it must at least be conceded that the possibility of an honest difference of opinion, or of sentiment, indicates that international equity is a dangerously elastic measure of national duty.

Trade in munitions of war seems to many objectionable; to some it seems immoral. It is repugnant to our feelings that men should enrich themselves by selling wares that are made to destroy their fellows. In international law, the shipment of military supplies from a neutral to a belligerent country appears to be regarded as an act neither illegitimate nor altogether legitimate. A neutral government may not itself furnish military supplies to a belligerent, but it is under no duty to prevent individuals within its jurisdiction from exporting such supplies. They do this, however, at their risk. Such supplies and the ships that carry them are subject to capture and forfeiture. In sanctioning such forfeiture, international law may be regarded as penalizing the trade. National law, on the other hand, treats this trade, in the absence of special restrictions, as legitimate. Our courts, state and federal, take cognizance of contracts for the sale and transportation of military supplies to belligerent countries and award damages if these contracts are not performed.[1]

The hope that a general prohibition of the sale of munitions of war to belligerents would promote peace seems to be groundless. Such a prohibition would increase armaments and might stimulate war. It would place unprepared nations, particularly those whose manufacturing industries are little developed, at the mercy of well-prepared nations, and particularly of those nations that have developed great manufacturing industries. For their own preservation, all non-industrial states would be forced to buy in time of peace and carry in stock military supplies of every sort sufficient to last through the longest war in which they might conceivably be involved. Much of this reserve would deteriorate; much would become relatively useless because of the progress of the military arts; and if a great industrial state should secretly develop and hold in readiness new and more effective agencies of destruction, as was the case before the outbreak of the present war, the non-industrial adversary, if shut out from neutral markets, would be unable to provide itself with the necessary equipment for defense. In view of these facts, it seems clear that the prohibition of the munitions trade in time of war would impair the rights of peaceful peoples. It might even imperil their independence.

In reply to the arguments of the Central Empires, our State Department did not fail to call attention to the fact that it had never been the policy of the United States to make extensive preparations for eventual war, and that, in any emergency, we were in the habit of relying upon purchase of military supplies from neutral states. It was, in fact, hardly intelligent diplomacy

[1] Kent, J., in Seton and Co. *v.* Low, 1 Johnson's N. Y. Cases, 1, 5, 6 (1799). Pond *v.* Smith, 4 Conn. 297, 303 (1822). Northern Pacific Railway Co. *v.* American Trading Co., 195 U. S. 439, 465 (1904).

on the part of the Central Empires to ask a nation so habitually unprepared as ours to set a precedent against trade in such supplies during war.

In the controversy aroused by its "war zone" proclamation, the German government, as we have seen, endeavored to connect the question of its right to conduct an unrestricted submarine warfare with the question of the trade in munitions of war. As we have seen, it argued that it was obliged to sink unarmed merchant vessels without warning in order to check this trade.[1] In invoking the right of reprisal, it sought to connect the question of submarine warfare with that of the British measures in restraint of neutral trade. It endeavored, for a time, to make action on the part of our government against Great Britain a condition precedent to any modification of its submarine warfare. At present, although it has ordered its submarine commanders to observe the rules of cruiser warfare, it has expressly reserved the right of reverting to its earlier policy of unrestricted submarine warfare, in case the United States does not succeed in inducing Great Britain to abandon its illegal restraint of neutral trade.

Our State Department has consistently refused to admit that the adjustment of any controversy between the United States and Germany can properly be made to depend on the adjustment of our controversies with any other power. It might have gone further; it might have said that there was no connection between the British restraints of neutral trade and the German policy of unrestricted submarine warfare, except that which the German government sought to establish by invoking the right of reprisal; and that the United States government did not recognize the taking of non-combatant lives as a proper or legitimate reprisal for the restriction of neutral trade.

The German government finds our position unneutral because we, as the German Ambassador at Washington asserts, have "acquiesced" in Great Britain's violations of international law. If protest without action or threat of action is acquiescence, it might equally well have been said, at the time of Count Bern-

[1] *Cf. supra*, pp. 503, 504.

storff's utterance and for many months afterward, that we had acquiesced in Germany's violations of international law.

To say that the United States is unneutral because it permits the export of military supplies to Germany's enemies, or because it has not compelled Great Britain to modify its Orders in Council, seems to most Americans absurd. To most of us it seems that our government has observed strict neutrality. In so far as the Central Empires and those who support their cause really feel that the attitude of the American government has not been neutral, their feeling is probably due to the fact that its observance of a strict neutrality has been of greater advantage to the Entente Allies than to the Central Empires. The fact that its conduct has given offence to both belligerent groups, and to those Americans whose sympathy with either group obscures their judgment, is the best proof that it has been really neutral.

Conclusions

The chief criticism that can be directed against our government is that it failed to discharge its full duty in protecting the rights of its citizens against those aggressions to which neutral rights are exposed in every war. Its greatest fault was in its lack of prevision; and particularly in its failure to arm itself at the outbreak of the war with the means of exercising naval force and economic pressure in support of its just claims. Lacking these means, it was condemned to inaction where action seemed requisite. It could not even threaten action, because its inability to take decisive action was notorious.

Minor faults, perhaps, but serious faults nevertheless, are to be found in the failure of our government to discover and to formulate the most tenable grounds for its protests and demands. For the development of international law this failure is most unfortunate; for international law, like every law that develops through precedents, depends for its certainty on the proper interpretation of precedents; and this is seriously compromised if the cases that may become precedents are not intelligently stated and argued.

MUNROE SMITH.

COLUMBIA UNIVERSITY.

Printed by Libri Plureos GmbH in Hamburg,
Germany